WHITE DRESSES

DR—To my girls in white dresses,
Melissa, Shannon, Natalie, and Kathryn

JH—For my family and my models

Text © 2006 Deborah Pace Rowley

Illustrations © 2006 Jewel Hodson

DESERET BOOK is a registered trademark of Deseret Book Company.

Visit us at DeseretBook.com

Library of Congress Cataloging-in-Publication Data
Rowley, Deborah Pace.
   White dresses : a baptism keepsake for girls / Deborah Rowley;
illustrated by Jewel Hodson.
      p. cm.
   ISBN-10 1-59038-632-9 (hardbound : alk. paper)
   ISBN-13 978-1-59038-632-3 (hardbound : alk. paper)
   1. Mormon girls—Religious life—Juvenile literature. 2. Mormon
women—Religious life—Juvenile literature. I. Hodson, Jewel. II. Title.
   BX8641.R69 2006
   242'.633—dc22   2006012729

Printed in China, 04/15
RR Donnelley, Shenzhen, China
10 9 8 7

WHITE DRESSES

BY DEBORAH PACE ROWLEY

ILLUSTRATED BY JEWEL HODSON

DESERET
BOOK

Salt Lake City, Utah

Today you were baptized. I waited for you in the baptismal font and took your hand to lead you into the water. You looked up at me. Your eyes were wide with nervous excitement. Then you gave me that dimpled grin that always melts my heart.

Suddenly I remembered your blessing day. You were wearing a special white dress, covered in ribbons and lace. You looked like an angel, sleeping with the tiniest smile on your face, as if you knew the most wonderful secret in the world. I looked down at you, gently cradled in my rough hands, and I thought to myself, *This is Heavenly Father's girl, and He has sent her to earth to me. I am so blessed to be her dad.*

Every day you bless my life. You taught me about love when you were two years old and wouldn't let go of your baby doll even to ride a pony. You were the best little mommy, carrying your baby around all day and snuggling with her at night.

You taught me about service when you were four and made me a birthday cake all by yourself. Wasn't Mom surprised when she came into the kitchen?

You taught me about repentance and forgiveness when you were six and I punished you for a rule you had broken. Afterwards, you ran into my arms and whispered through your tears, "I'm sorry, Daddy. I want to be good."

Today you taught me about the plan of salvation. I took your hand and you held my wrist the way we had practiced. I said the sacred words of the baptismal prayer and lowered you into the water. When you came out of the water you were so clean and innocent, I could have hugged you there in the font forever. I rejoiced that through the atonement of Christ and repentance you can always be that way.

Mom helped you change out of your wet clothes. She brushed your hair and tied it up with a new white ribbon. Your shiny face glowed with happiness as you came out of the dressing room to meet me. Your pretty white dress symbolized just how clean you were inside.

I placed my hands on your head and used the priesthood to confirm you a member of The Church of Jesus Christ of Latter-day Saints and bestow upon you the gift of the Holy Ghost. I felt the Spirit whisper how wonderful you are and how much your Heavenly Father loves you. I hope that is something you never forget.

You will need the Holy Ghost to help you every day. I want to teach you how to recognize the warm, happy feelings of the Spirit when we read the scriptures, have family home evening, and say family prayer. The Holy Ghost will help you keep the Word of Wisdom and stay morally clean. If you listen to the Spirit, you will be guided when I'm not there to protect you.

Remember when you were sick last summer? Mom put cool cloths on your forehead and let you eat grape popsicles in bed. I gave you a father's blessing by the power of the priesthood. I want to be worthy to give you a blessing every time you need one—anytime you're sick or hurting or confused or afraid.

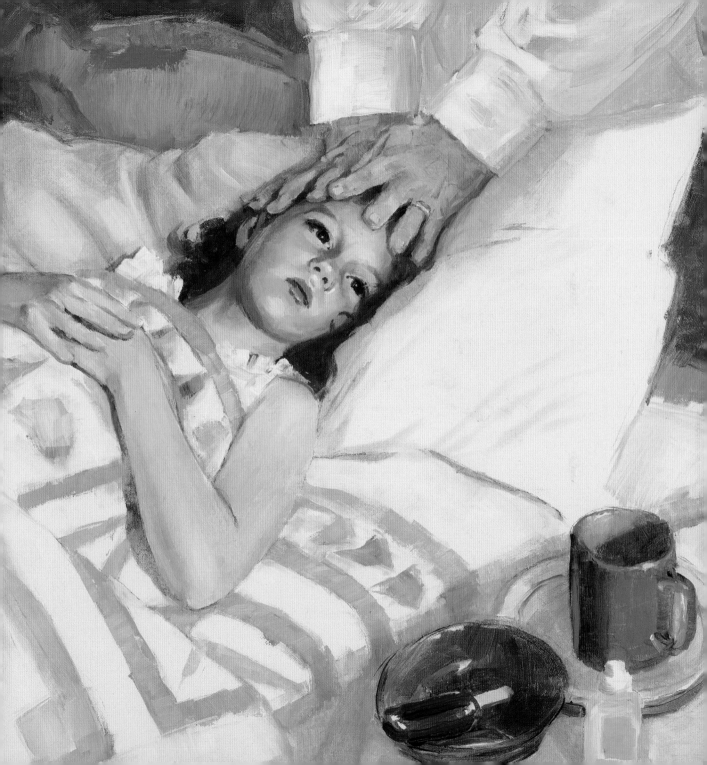

I can't wait until you're twelve. You'll wake up early in the morning to do baptisms for the dead. You'll walk into the temple and feel a special spirit because it is the House of the Lord. The temple is so beautiful with everyone dressed in white, and going to the temple to perform sacred ordinances will increase your desire to stay worthy and clean.

Before I know it, you'll be a teenager. You will mess up the bathroom with makeup, mess up your room with clothes, maybe even mess up my car with a fender bender. If you ever make a big mess of things and need to repent, the atonement of the Savior can make things right again. Remember I love you, no matter what, messes and all.

I'll love you even when you go on a date with a boy besides me. I can picture a nervous young man coming to get you for a dance. I will have to talk with him just a little to make sure he treats you right. You will enter the room looking so pretty in a modest dress that will take my breath away. That won't be the only time I'll feel like bragging because you're mine. Recitals, concerts, games, graduation. Whatever you do, I'll be there to cheer you on.

One day you'll come home to tell us you're in love. Every day I pray that you'll be led to a worthy priesthood holder who will treat you like the daughter of God you are. When that day comes, I'll feel excited and a little sad at the same time because my baby girl will be all grown up. You'll enter the temple and put on another white dress, even more beautiful than the ones you have worn before.

In the temple, you will kneel across the altar from your eternal companion. I will listen as you are sealed together for time and all eternity. Your beautiful white dress will remind your husband that you can become a queen and that as he loves you and honors you, you will reign at his side forever. In the temple I'll look back and see what a blessing you have been to your dad all your life. Our eyes will meet, and I'll start to cry.

One wonderful day, if we both are faithful, I will wait for you in heaven. You will return to your Heavenly Father, clean and pure, dressed in white again. The trials of life will be forgotten as I pull you into my arms. The very first time I held you, I felt like a king.

I love you, Princess. Thank you for being baptized. I can't wait for the rest of your life.